MORE KENTUCKY BOURBON COCKTAILS

MORE

KENTUCKY BOURBON

COCKTAILS

Joy Perrine and Susan Reigler

Photographs by Jessica Ebelhar

University Press of Kentucky

Editorial and Sales Offices: The University Press of Kentucky
663 South Limestone Street, Lexington, Kentucky 40508-4008
www.kentuckypress.com

Library of Congress Cataloging-in-Publication Data

Names: Perrine, Joy, author. | Reigler, Susan, author.
Title: More Kentucky bourbon cocktails / Joy Perrine and Susan Reigler ;
photographs by Jessica Ebelhar.
Description: Lexington, Kentucky : University Press of Kentucky, [2016] |
Includes index.
Identifiers: LCCN 2016021465| ISBN 9780813167688 (hardcover : alk. paper) |
ISBN 9780813168104 (pdf) | ISBN 9780813168098 (epub)
Subjects: LCSH: Cocktails. | Bourbon whiskey. | Whiskey. | LCGFT: Cookbooks.
Classification: LCC TX951 .P47424 2016 | DDC 641.87/4—dc23 LC record available
at https://lccn.loc.gov/2016021465

This book is printed on acid-free paper meeting
the requirements of the American National Standard
for Permanence in Paper for Printed Library Materials.

Manufactured in the United States of America.

Member of the Association of American University Presses

CONTENTS

Photographs follow page 40

PREFACE

The original *Kentucky Bourbon Cocktail Book*, published in 2009, is now in its fifth printing. We knew, given the rising tide of bourbon's popularity, that it would be a hit. Perhaps most gratifying is how popular bourbon cocktails have become, not just in Kentucky but around the country.

For this sequel to our first cocktail book, Joy has added many more of her own recipes, and Susan has gathered others from Louisville's leading bartenders. We have also included winning drinks from several popular cocktail contests and have handpicked a baker's dozen recipes from our friend Albert Schmid's *The Kentucky Bourbon Cookbook* that we know will make a great menu for a party. Yes, we've matched four of Joy's new cocktails to that menu, too.

Chapter 1 of *The Kentucky Bourbon Cocktail Book* described the equipment needed to set up your home bar. We hope that if you have picked up this book, it's because you already have a copy of the first. But in case you don't, we have included an adapted excerpt from that chapter as an appendix to get your home bar up and running.

Several recipes in this volume call for some specialty ingredients from Bourbon Barrel Foods and Kilimanjaro Foods, both Louisville-based companies. Their products are widely available in Kentucky, but if you live outside the Bluegrass State, you

can visit each company's website to order ingredients—http://bourbonbarrelfoods
.com and http://www.kfoodsinc.com.

As in our first volume, drinks have been chosen with the home cocktail maker in mind. We tried to keep them simple. We also encourage you to experiment and use bourbon to invent your own recipes. Happy mixing!

Joy's Recipes

THE BIG KENTUCKY BOURBON BRANDS

Yes, 95 percent of the world's bourbon comes from Kentucky. Aside from a tiny amount made by a handful of craft distillers, this whiskey bounty flows from just nine major distilleries. The following recipes have been created to showcase the flavor profiles of a product from each of the Big Nine.

.

THE BARDSTOWN COCKTAIL—
BARTON 1792 DISTILLERY (BARDSTOWN)

We spend time every year at the Kentucky Bourbon Festival in Bardstown, Kentucky, where we present a program called Bourbon Cocktail Mixology. Joy demonstrates how to make a cocktail using products from each of the sponsoring distilleries, and Susan provides unique facts about each. The venue for the event is virtually next door to the Barton 1792 Distillery (http://www.1792bourbon.com).

2 ounces 1792 Ridgemont Reserve
1/2 ounce Red Dubonnet
1/2 ounce White Dubonnet
4 dashes Fee Brothers West Indian orange bitters

Combine and shake over ice. Strain into a chilled cocktail glass and garnish with an orange wedge.

PINEAPPLE PUNCH—BROWN-FORMAN
DISTILLERY (LOUISVILLE)

When Joy does events for nonprofit organizations such as Louisville's Filson Historical Society, this is her go-to punch for a crowd. Old Forester was the first brand of bourbon to be sold exclusively in bottles, in 1870 (http://www.oldforester.com).

2 ounces Old Forester

1 ounce brown sugar syrup

$1/8$ teaspoon ground nutmeg

4 ounces pineapple juice

Combine in a pint glass over ice and shake. Add a splash of sparkling wine and a sprinkling of nutmeg. Garnish with a cube of fresh pineapple.

HOO DOO COCKTAIL—BUFFALO TRACE DISTILLERY (FRANKFORT)

Joy was inspired to create this cocktail on a trip to Tales of the Cocktail in New Orleans in 2012. Buffalo Trace (http://www.buffalotracedistillery.com) is owned by the Sazerac Company, which is based in New Orleans—and, of course, pecan-flavored praline is a signature sweet of the Big Easy.

2 ounces Buffalo Trace bourbon

1 ounce praline liqueur

1 ounce Buffalo Trace Bourbon Cream

Combine and shake over ice. Strain into a chilled cocktail glass swirled with caramel sauce and a sprinkling of fresh ground cinnamon.

BLACKBERRY CORDIAL—FOUR ROSES DISTILLERY (LAWRENCEBURG)

This is one of the drinks Joy makes for Bourbon Cocktail Mixology. You can also strain the ingredients into two chilled cocktail glasses for a refreshing cocktail. Find information about the distillery at http://fourrosesbourbon.com.

4 ounces blackberry-infused Four Roses Yellow Label
1 ounce sorghum
1 ounce Kilimanjaro Foods ginger syrup
1 ounce Smucker's blackberry syrup
1 ounce Kentucky Blackberry wine

Combine and shake over ice and strain into 4 3-ounce cordial glasses. Drop a fresh blackberry into each.

To make the infusion, combine 1 liter of Four Roses Yellow Label with 1 pint of fresh blackberries in a clean glass jar large enough to hold the ingredients. Leave on a shelf at room temperature for 4 days. Strain into a second glass container. Date and store in refrigerator, where it will last about 2 weeks.

GINGER SNAP—HEAVEN HILL DISTILLERY (LOUISVILLE)

Joy's introduction to Kentucky bourbon was in St. Croix, U.S. Virgin Islands, in the late 1970s. She drank Old Fitzgerald Prime with ginger ale and a squeeze of lemon. She was inspired to create the Ginger Snap when Kilimanjaro Foods released its ginger syrup. To find more information about Old Fitzgerald, go to http://heavenhill.com/brand/21.

2 ounces Old Fitzgerald Prime

¾ ounce brown sugar syrup

½ ounce Kilimanjaro Foods ginger syrup

1 ounce fresh lemon juice

Shake over ice and strain into a chilled cocktail glass. Add a splash of ginger ale. Garnish with a lemon wedge.

DEVIL IN A BLUE DRESS—JIM BEAM DISTILLERY (CLERMONT)

Joy couldn't resist creating this cocktail when Beam released Devil's Cut (http://www .jimbeam.com/devils-cut/about-devils-cut). The name signals the opposite of the Angels' share, the whiskey that evaporates from barrels as they are aging. After the barrel is dumped for bottling, some bourbon is left soaked into the wood. Beam extracts this whiskey from the wood and adds it to the bourbon it bottles as the Devil's Cut.

2 ounces Jim Beam Devil's Cut

1 ounce Triple Sec

2 ounces Ocean Spray blueberry juice

Shake over ice and strain into a chilled cocktail glass. Garnish with an orange slice.

GRAPEFRUIT OLD FASHIONED—MAKER'S MARK (LORETTO)

Joy says, "This cocktail reminds me of the broiled grapefruit I ate as a child. The spicy notes in Maker's Mark make the flavors pop."

2 ounces Maker's Mark
1 ounce brown sugar syrup
4 dashes Fee Brothers grapefruit bitters
1 wedge pink grapefruit
1 cherry
1 ounce water

Lightly muddle fruit, bitters, and syrup in an Old Fashioned glass. Add Maker's Mark, water, and ice. Shake and enjoy.

HONEY BERRY—WILD TURKEY (LAWRENCEBURG)

This is a very refreshing summer cocktail!

1 ounce Wild Turkey American Honey
1 ounce Russell's Reserve
1 tablespoon simple syrup
3 ounces fresh orange juice

Shake over ice and strain into a chilled cocktail glass. Drizzle with blackberry syrup and garnish with a blackberry and fresh mint.

CHERRY MANHATTAN—WOODFORD RESERVE (VERSAILLES)

Joy's take on a classic Manhattan takes advantage of the excellent cherry flavor in the Woodford Spiced Cherry Bitters made by Bourbon Barrel Foods.

3 ounces Woodford Reserve
4 dashes Woodford Reserve Spiced Cherry Bitters
1 ounce Kentucky cherry wine

Combine over ice. Shake and strain into a chilled cocktail glass. Garnish with a fresh, pitted cherry.

HOLIDAY COCKTAIL—ANY OF THE BIG NINE

Cranberries and oranges are the flavors of Christmas and make a great cocktail combination. Any one of the premium bourbons in this section will work well in this drink. Experiment to find your favorite!

2 ounces Kentucky bourbon
½ ounce brown sugar syrup
3 dashes Fee Brothers West Indian orange bitters
3 dashes Fee Brothers cranberry bitters
1 ounce Grand Marnier
2 ounces Kentucky cranberry wine

Combine and shake over ice. Strain into a chilled cocktail glass and garnish with an orange wedge on the rim.

JULEPS

The Kentucky Derby season starts in April. That means it's julep-drinking season, too. Every year, Four Roses Distillery sponsors a mint julep recipe contest. (See one winning recipe on pp. 49–50.) Joy has a mint julep dinner at Equus Restaurant and Jack's Lounge with Woodford Reserve and Brown-Forman master distiller Chris Morris. Chris brings one of the $1,000 mint julep cups that are sold to raise money for Thoroughbred horse charities.

The crucial ingredient for a great julep—in addition, of course, to good bourbon—is the syrup. This recipe can be used for any of the juleps herein:

KENTUCKY MINT SYRUP

2 cups boiling water

2 cups cane sugar

2 cups Kentucky Colonel mint leaves

Add mint leaves to boiling water. Boil 2 minutes. Add sugar, boil 1 minute. Cover pot and remove from heat. Steep 6 hours or overnight. Strain, bottle, and refrigerate. Keeps approximately 1 week.

JOY'S MINT JULEP

2 ounces Kentucky bourbon

1 ounce mint syrup

6–8 mint leaves

Add syrup and mint leaves to the glass and muddle the leaves. Then add bourbon and 1 ounce of water. Fill with crushed ice. Garnish with a large sprig of mint.

PINEAPPLE JULEP

2 ounces Kentucky bourbon

1 ounce pineapple juice

1 ounce mint syrup

3 tablespoons chopped fresh pineapple

6 Kentucky Colonel mint leaves

Combine syrup, mint leaves, and pineapple in the julep cup and muddle. Add crushed ice to fill. Then add the bourbon and the pineapple juice. Garnish with fresh mint and a pineapple spear, then serve with a long straw.

STRAWBERRY JULEP

2 ounces Kentucky bourbon
1 ounce mint syrup
3 chopped strawberries
6 Kentucky Colonel mint leaves

Combine syrup, mint leaves, and strawberries in the julep cup and muddle.
Add crushed ice to fill. Then add the bourbon and 1 ounce of water. Garnish with
fresh mint and a strawberry and serve with a long straw.

FROZEN MINT JULEP

This is especially good on a very hot and humid day.

$\frac{1}{2}$ cup mint syrup
1 cup Kentucky bourbon
$\frac{1}{4}$ cup mint leaves

Pour all ingredients into a blender. Add ice to fill. Blend. Pour into a cup or glass
and garnish with a sprig of mint.

CHOCOLATE JULEP

2 ounces Kentucky bourbon

1 ounce white crème de menthe

1 ounce dark crème de cacao

Shake over ice. Pour into a chilled cocktail glass and garnish with a mint sprig or, even better, a chocolate mint sprig.

THE OLD FASHIONED—THEME AND VARIATIONS

The Old Fashioned cocktail as we know it today traces its roots to Louisville's private Pendennis Club. It is still, by far, the most-mixed cocktail at the club. The house bourbon is Old Forester, so it (or its sibling, Woodford Reserve) is recommended in these recipes. But feel free to substitute bourbons of similar proof. The only exception is the recipe calling for Woodford Reserve Double Oaked, which has such a unique flavor profile that it would be difficult to find a good substitute. (Not that Old Forester and Woodford aren't distinctive bourbons, too.)

CLASSIC OLD FASHIONED

2 ounces Old Forester Signature (100 proof)

½ ounce simple sugar syrup

6 dashes Angostura bitters

1 orange wedge—squeeze and drop

1 cherry—squeeze and drop

Combine syrup, orange, cherry, and bitters in the glass. Add bourbon and 1 ounce of water, then add ice and shake. Garnish with a large lemon twist.

STRAWBERRY RHUBARB OLD FASHIONED

2 ounces Old Forester (86 proof)

1 ounce strawberry syrup (Smucker's works well)

2 chopped strawberries

6–8 dashes Fee Brothers rhubarb bitters

Combine syrup, fruit, and bitters in the glass and lightly muddle. Add bourbon, ice, and 1 ounce of water. Shake. Garnish with a strawberry on the rim.

PINEAPPLE PLUM OLD FASHIONED

2 ounces Old Forester (86 proof)

1 ounce pineapple juice

1 ounce Kilimanjaro Foods brown sugar syrup

6 dashes Fee Brothers plum bitters

3 cubes fresh pineapple

1 wedge fresh plum, if available

Combine syrup and fruit in the glass and lightly muddle. Add ice, bourbon, and juice. Shake and garnish with a pineapple wedge.

BLUEBERRY ORANGE OLD FASHIONED

2 ounces Woodford Reserve (90.4 proof)

1 ounce blueberry syrup (Smucker's works well)

6 dashes Fee Brothers West Indian orange bitters

6–8 blueberries

1 orange wedge—squeeze and drop

Combine syrup and fruit in the glass and lightly muddle. Add bourbon, 1 ounce of water, and ice. Shake. Garnish with an orange twist.

NEW FASHIONED #2

2 ounces Woodford Reserve (90.4 proof)

1 ounce Kilimanjaro Foods ginger syrup

2 lemon wedges—squeeze and drop

1 cherry

4 dashes Angostura bitters

4 dashes Fee Brothers lemon bitters

Splash Korbel (or other) sparkling wine

Combine syrup, fruit, and bitters in the glass. Add ice and bourbon. Shake. Then add a splash of sparkling wine. Garnish with a lemon twist.

CHERRY OAK OLD FASHIONED

2 ounces Woodford Reserve Double Oaked

1 ounce Kilimanjaro Foods brown sugar syrup

3 Bourbon Barrel Foods Woodford Reserve cherries

4–6 dashes Bourbon Barrel Foods Woodford Reserve Spiced Cherry Bitters

Combine syrup, fruit, and bitters in the glass. Lightly muddle. Add ice, bourbon, and a splash of juice from the jar of cherries. Shake and garnish with a cherry.

PEACH OLD FASHIONED

For this refreshing summer drink, use the ripest, sweetest peaches you can find.
Those from Trimble County, Kentucky, are notably good.

2 ounces Kentucky bourbon
1 ounce brown sugar syrup
1 ounce Kilimanjaro Foods ginger syrup
4 fresh peach slices, peeled
2 fresh pitted cherries

Combine all ingredients, except the bourbon, in the glass and muddle. Then add the bourbon, enough ice to fill the glass, and top off with water (about 1 ounce).

FRUIT MANHATTANS

The classic Manhattan cocktail is made with whiskey, vermouth, and bitters. Vermouth is a fortified wine, so these recipes offer a little twist on the classic by using Kentucky wines in place of the vermouth. While you are probably aware that 95 percent of the world's bourbon is made in Kentucky, you may not know that the state was home to the first commercial winery and the first professional vintners' association in the United States. There are seventy wineries in the state today, producing bottles ranging from sweet to dry. For a complete list of wineries and their products, go to http://www.kentuckywine.com. In addition to many made with grapes, a lot of Kentucky wines are made with other fruits. If you live outside of Kentucky, check your local wine shop for fruit wines from your region to use in these recipes. These recipes employ many different flavors of bitters, too. The basic recipe will be:

2 ounces Kentucky bourbon
4 dashes bitters
1 ounce Kentucky fruit or honey wine

Combine over ice. Shake and strain into a chilled cocktail glass and garnish.
Always use Kentucky bourbon, then try these Manhattan variations:

Wine	*Bitters*	*Garnish*
Honey	Lemon	Large lemon twist
Strawberry	Rhubarb	Large strawberry
Cherry	Cherry	Pitted fresh cherry
Peach	Peach	Peach slice
Plum	Plum	Plum slice
Cranberry	Cranberry	Orange twist
Blackberry	West Indian orange	Orange wheel/blackberry
Blueberry	Lemon	Lemon twist/5 blueberries

Now that you know the basic recipe, have some fun and create your own fruit Manhattans!

WARM WEATHER REFRESHERS

ORANGE DROP

2 ounces Kentucky bourbon
½ ounce brown sugar syrup
2 ounces fresh-squeezed orange juice
4 dashes Fee Brothers West Indian orange bitters

Shake over ice and strain into a chilled cocktail glass. Garnish with a candied orange slice.

You can make your own brown sugar syrup by dissolving 2 cups of light brown sugar in 1 cup of boiling water. After it cools, bottle and date it. It will keep, refrigerated, for 2 weeks. Or you can use Kilimanjaro Foods brown sugar syrup.

SUMMER MANHATTAN

3 ounces Kentucky bourbon
1 ounce white wine
4 dashes Fee Brothers West Indian orange bitters
1 ounce fresh-squeezed orange juice

Combine over ice, shake, and strain into a chilled cocktail glass. Garnish with a large orange twist.

KENTUCKY SUMMER FRUIT PUNCH

This recipe makes about half a gallon of punch, so it's great for a party where you want a signature cocktail. Be sure to use fresh, ripe fruit.

1 liter Kentucky bourbon
1 cup brown sugar syrup
1 12-ounce can frozen pink lemonade concentrate, thawed

Combine liquids in a large punch bowl and whisk together.
Add:

1 cup blueberries
1 cup chopped pineapple
1 cup sliced strawberries
1 cup chopped peaches

Add 1 750-ml bottle of sparkling wine. Stir to combine and ladle into ice-filled cups. Include some fruit in each.

KENTUCKY SANGRIA

12 ounces Kentucky bourbon
½ cup brown sugar
½ cup Triple Sec
1 750-ml bottle red wine made in Kentucky
1 12-ounce can defrosted pink lemonade (do not add water)

Combine in a pitcher and stir well. Add orange wheels, lemon wheels, sliced strawberries, and green grapes. Serve over ice in wineglasses and include some fruit in each drink.

SOUTHERN SANGRITA

Sangrita (not to be confused with sangria!) is often served as a chaser to a shot of tequila. Bourbon is substituted to make a single drink. Warning: You may breathe a little fire after drinking this.

2 ounces Kentucky bourbon
1 ounce brown sugar syrup
1 ounce fresh orange juice
1 ounce tomato juice
1 ounce fresh lime juice
1 ounce jalapeño pepper juice

Combine over ice and shake. Pour into a glass and garnish with an orange wheel, a lime wedge, and a small, fresh jalapeño pepper or pepper slice.

WATERMELON SLUSH

This is the perfect cooler for a hot Kentucky summer afternoon.

2 ounces Kentucky bourbon
1 ounce simple syrup
1 ounce fresh lime juice
3 watermelon cubes

Combine in blender with ice. Blend and pour into 2 glasses. Garnish with a small watermelon wedge or lime wheel.

PINK BERRY

This is a festive and colorful cooler for a midsummer picnic!

½ liter dried strawberry-infused Kentucky bourbon (80–90 proof)
12-ounce can frozen pink lemonade concentrate, thawed
3 12-ounce cans ginger ale

Combine ingredients in a 2-quart glass pitcher and stir. Add 10–12 lemon wheel slices and 10–12 cleaned, hulled, and sliced fresh strawberries. Let sit about 30 minutes. Serve over ice and garnish with half a strawberry and a sprig of mint.

Here's how to infuse the bourbon:

1 liter Kentucky bourbon

6–8 ounces dried strawberries (available at Whole Foods and other specialty stores)

Pour bourbon into a half-gallon jar and add dried strawberries. Put on the lid and give the jar a good shake. Let it rest on shelf or counter for 3 days. Strain through fine-mesh strainer lined with cheesecloth into a clean glass jar. Label, date, and store. It does not need to be refrigerated, but use within a week.

COCKTAILS USING BOURBON-BASED PRODUCTS

In recent years many distilleries have released whiskies infused with flavorings. By law, only distilled water can be added to bourbon to adjust its proof. Nothing can be added to bourbon to change its color or flavor. So once a flavoring is added, the whiskey is no longer technically "bourbon." Whatever their designations, these products have been very popular and can be the basis for some very enjoyable cocktails.

BLUEBERRY TWIST

2 ounces Evan Williams Honey Reserve

1 ounce Kentucky bourbon

1 ounce brown sugar syrup

1 ounce fresh lemon juice

1 ounce Ocean Spray blueberry juice

Combine over ice and shake. Drop in 5 blueberries and a large lemon twist to garnish.

In addition to the honey flavor, Heaven Hill has two other flavored expressions of Evan Williams: cinnamon and cherry.

BLACK CHERRY BOUNCE

Cherry bounce was a homemade cordial popular on the early American frontier. This is an updated version. Other Red Stag flavors are maple and cinnamon.

3 ounces Jim Beam Red Stag black cherry
1 ounce brown sugar syrup
2 ounces Ocean Spray cherry juice

Combine over ice and shake. Drop 3 fresh, pitted cherries in for garnish.

KENTUCKY ICED COFFEE

Buffalo Trace Bourbon Cream will make you forget all about other cream-based liqueurs. Try a shot of it in hot coffee during the winter. When you tour the distillery in Frankfort, the guides offer a tasting of "the best root beer float you've ever had," which is the bourbon cream added to root beer. Highly recommended.

2 ounces Kentucky bourbon
1 ounce Kahlúa
2 ounces Buffalo Trace Bourbon Cream
4 ounces cooled strong coffee

Combine over ice and shake. Top with fresh whipped cream, grated fresh cinnamon, and a cherry.

KENTUCKY COFFEE COCKTAIL

Angel's Envy is aged in port wine barrels, which gives it a very winelike finish. This is based on a historic recipe that used brandy instead of bourbon. The cocktail separates into layers and looks like coffee: hence the name.

2 ounces Angel's Envy
2 ounces port wine
1 egg (whirled in a blender to mix the white and yolk)

Combine over ice and shake until thoroughly mixed. Strain into a chilled champagne flute.

HONEY OF A MANHATTAN

If you like the Scotch-based liqueur Drambuie, you will love American Honey. Enjoyable on its own, it is especially good with a squeeze of lemon.

2 ounces Wild Turkey American Honey
½ ounce Wild Turkey 101
½ ounce fresh lemon juice
6 dashes Fee Brothers lemon bitters
1 ounce Kentucky honey wine

Combine and shake over ice. Strain into a chilled cocktail glass. Garnish by floating a thin lemon wheel on top.

PEACH SURPRISE

There's actually some Kentucky bourbon in Southern Comfort, which is owned by the New Orleans–based Sazerac Company. That's the "surprise."

2 ounces Kentucky bourbon
½ ounce brown sugar syrup
½ ounce Southern Comfort
3 ounces Ocean Spray White Cran-Peach Juice
5 peeled, sliced peaches

Combine all ingredients, including the peach slices, over ice and shake. Garnish with 3 fresh, pitted cherries and serve with a straw.

BOURBON TRUFFLE

1 ½ ounces Kentucky bourbon

½ ounce Tuaca

½ ounce dark crème de cacao

1 ½ ounces Buffalo Trace Bourbon Cream

Pour bourbon, Tuaca, and crème de cacao over ice and shake. Strain into a chilled cocktail glass. Carefully pour the Buffalo Trace Bourbon Cream into the center. The drink will separate into layers.

CHAPTER TWO

On (and Off) Louisville's Urban Bourbon Trail

The success of the Kentucky Bourbon Trail, which includes several of the state's major distilleries, inspired the city of Louisville to create its own Urban Bourbon Trail (UBT) in 2009. The trail originally had eight stops. As of 2015, it boasted thirty restaurants and bars. In order to be a designated stop, an establishment must serve at least fifty different bourbons, have a certain number of dishes on its menu that use bourbon as an ingredient, and offer creative bourbon-based cocktails.

Considering that one-third of the world's bourbon is distilled in Louisville, you can imagine that the city is a center for lots of innovative bourbon mixology. This is thanks to the presence of two large distilleries, Brown-Forman, maker of Old Forester, and Heaven Hill's Bernheim Distillery, where brands including Evan Williams, Elijah Craig, Heaven Hill, Old Fitzgerald, and other bourbons are made. Naturally, these "hometown bourbons" are featured frequently in the Louisville recipes. Woodford Reserve, distilled near Versailles and also owned by Brown-Forman, is used frequently, too.

This section contains recipes from UBT bartenders, some flavorful drinks enjoyed at non-UBT establishments, and even a couple of cocktails from a nonprofessional bourbon enthusiast and from a non-Kentucky distillery. (Yes, *quite* a way off the UBT.) Urban Bourbon Trail members are identified by the designation UBT next to the restaurant name.

For more information about the Urban Bourbon Trail and a complete list of restaurants and bars, go to http://www.bourboncountry.com/things-to-do/urban-bourbon-trail/index.aspx.

THE BAR AT BLU (UBT)

BLU Italian Grille (in the downtown Louisville Marriott)
280 West Jefferson St. | 502-671-4285 | www.blugrille.com

RICK HOUSE NAIL

This easy-sipping drink is mellow and smoky.

1½ ounces Evan Williams Single Barrel
Splash Kahlúa
Splash Drambuie

Add all ingredients to the snifter, stir gently, and add only 2 ice cubes.

BOURBONS BISTRO (UBT)

2255 Frankfort Ave. | *502-894-8838* | *www.bourbonsbistro.com*

MAPLE BACON OLD FASHIONED

Bourbons Bistro carries a selection of more than 130 American whiskies. The bar and restaurant together have been named an "Icon of Whisky" by Britain's Whisky Magazine.

2–3 ounces Knob Creek Maple bourbon
Slice orange
1 cherry
Dash maple bitters
½ ounce bacon simple syrup

In the bottom of the glass, muddle the orange and cherry with the bacon simple syrup. Fill the glass with ice and top with the whiskey.

To make the bacon simple syrup, add 1 teaspoon of bacon fat and 1 ounce of sugar to 1 ounce of warm water. Allow to steep for several minutes. Then strain through a coffee filter and use.

CHARR'D BOURBON KITCHEN & LOUNGE (UBT)

Louisville Marriott East, 1903 Embassy Square Blvd. | 502-491-1184
www.marriott.com/hotels/hotel-information/restaurant/sdfls-louisville-marriott-east/

CHARR'D BLACKBERRY MANHATTAN

Recipe provided by Bonnie Eisert of the Louisville Marriott East, a bourbon-themed hotel that is the official hotel of the Kentucky Bourbon Trail.

1½ ounces Jim Beam Red Stag
½ ounce Grand Marnier
3 blackberries
1 cherry

Add fruit to a cocktail shaker and muddle well. Add ice, Grand Marnier, and Red Stag. Shake well and strain into a chilled cocktail glass. Garnish with a blackberry.

DISH ON MARKET (UBT)

434 West Market St. | 502-315-0669 | www.dishonmarket.com

FORESTER 75

Dish proprietor Anderson Grissom explained that this is a Kentucky version of the classic French 75, which uses gin. It's a very quick and easy cocktail to make.

1 ounce Old Forester
½ ounce simple syrup
Lemon wedge
Korbel Brut Rose

Add the bourbon and syrup to the champagne glass and ream the lip of the glass with the lemon wedge. Fill with the sparkling wine, add a squeeze of lemon, and serve.

DOC CROW'S SOUTHERN SMOKEHOUSE & RAW BAR

127 West Main St. | 502-587-1626 | www.doccrows.com

DOC CROW'S MINT JULEP LEMONADE

Doc Crow's, named in honor of bourbon pioneer Dr. James Crow, is located in the block of Main Street known as Whiskey Row, which was home in the nineteenth century to numerous distillery warehouses and offices. This cocktail is the creation of beverage director Jackie Zykan.

1 ounce Elijah Craig 12-Year-Old Small Batch
1 ounce fresh lemonade
1 ounce simple syrup
1 ounce water
8–10 mint leaves

Mix the ingredients in a cocktail shaker and muddle the mint. Fill with ice and shake vigorously. Strain into an ice-filled tall glass and garnish with a mint sprig.

DOWN ONE BOURBON BAR & RESTAURANT (UBT)

321 West Main St. | 502-566-3259 | www.downonebourbonbar.com

HELLER IN PINK TIGHTS

This drink takes full advantage of the classic fruity notes in bourbon.

2 ounces Ancient Age

1 ounce Aperol

½ ounce fresh lemon juice

½ ounce simple syrup

Shake all ingredients together. Strain into a mason jar over crushed ice. Top with San Pellegrino blood orange soda. Garnish with lemon straws.

LILLYS—A KENTUCKY BISTRO (UBT)

1147 Bardstown Rd. | *502-451-0447* | *www.lillysbistro.com*

BEAM ME UP, SCOTTY!

This cocktail was invented by owner/chef Kathy Cary's son Will Cary Jr. and bartender Josh McDevitt for a special outer space–themed dinner benefiting astronomy education at a local public school. Kathy came up with the name. Who knew bourbon and Scotch could be so compatible? But then, the starship Enterprise *had an impressively multicultural crew, so perhaps this isn't so surprising after all.*

1 ounce Jim Beam White Label
1 ounce Glenmorangie
¾ ounce Drambuie
Crabbie's ginger beer

Combine bourbon, Scotch, and Drambuie in the glass and stir. Fill with ice and top with the ginger beer.

PROOF ON MAIN (UBT)

702 West Main St. | 502-217-6360 | www.proofonmain.com

BULLEIT-VARDIER

This variation on the classic Boulevardier was created by Proof on Main's bartender, January Miller. The bar and restaurant are located in the 21c Museum Hotel, a showcase for contemporary art owned by Brown-Forman bourbon heiress Laura Lee Brown and her husband, Steve Wilson.

1½ ounces Bulleit bourbon
¾ ounce Aperol
¾ ounce Fonseca Port
2 dashes Fee's Old Fashioned Bitters

Add all ingredients to a mixing beaker with crushed ice. Stir and strain into the coupe glass. Garnish with orange peel.

RAMSI'S CAFÉ ON THE WORLD (UBT)

1293 Bardstown Rd. | 502-451-0700 | www.ramsiscafe.com

THE KENTUCKY SHAMAN

Rhona Bowles Kamar, chef/owner of Ramsi's, provided the background for this drink: "Growing up in the woods of Kentucky with a 'witch doctor' for a mother, I have many memories of her concoctions and unorthodox healing techniques. Her cure for a winter cough was peppermint candy soaked in bourbon, the inspiration for this drink."

1½ ounces Four Roses Single Barrel
¼ inch peeled, fresh ginger
1 tablespoon raw, local honey

Add hot water to the snifter to warm it. Then discard the water. Put honey in the snifter, grate the ginger into it, and half-fill the glass with hot water; stir. Add the bourbon and garnish with a whole peppermint stick.

SEVICHE—A LATIN RESTAURANT

1538 Bardstown Rd. | 502-473-8560 | www.severestaurant.com

KENTUCKY MOJITO

Chef Anthony Lamas enlivens his creative Latin American menu with a few southern touches. So it's natural to find bourbon in place of rum in his restaurant's mojito.

2–3 ounces Kentucky bourbon
1 teaspoon sugar
½ lime
Pinch of mint
Soda water
Sour mix

In the bottom of the pint glass, muddle sugar, mint, and lime in a splash of soda water. Add bourbon and ice and sour mix to fill. Stir and serve.

211 CLOVER LANE RESTAURANT

211 Clover Ln. | 502-896-9570 | www.211clover.com

THE WOODFORD RICKHOUSE

Emily Hornback, the bar manager at 211 Clover, named this drink in honor of the flavors present in the rickhouses (or bourbon warehouses) dotted throughout central Kentucky: from the wood of the oak barrels in which the bourbon is aged to the wildflowers pollinated by bees storing their honey in nearby hives.

1½ ounces Woodford Reserve Double Oaked
1 ounce Dolin Blanc French vermouth infused with chamomile, vanilla bean, and honey herbal tea
2 dashes Woodford sorghum and vanilla bean bitters
Vanilla bean dry soda water

Combine bourbon, vermouth, sorghum, and bitters in the glass and stir. Fill with ice and top off with the soda water. Garnish with a long lemon twist.

UPTOWN CAFÉ

1624 Bardstown Rd. | 502-458-4212 | www.uptownlouisville.com

KENTUCKY GIMLET

There's a wonderful tartness to this cocktail, which is especially refreshing in warm weather. Thanks to Uptown owner Kelley Ledford for the recipe, which was created by bartender Evan Blanford.

5 ounces Evan Williams Single Barrel
1 ounce fresh lime juice
1 ounce simple syrup
4–5 fresh basil leaves

Chill a 9-ounce cocktail glass with ice and water, and set aside. Add the lime juice, syrup, and basil leaves to a shaker and muddle. Then add the bourbon and some ice and shake well. Discard the ice and water from the cocktail glass and strain the mixture into it. Garnish with a lime slice.

VILLAGE ANCHOR PUB & ROOST (UBT)

11507 Park Rd. | 502-708-1850 | www.villageanchor.com

BROWN SUGAR OLD FASHIONED

Even though it's not muddled, as so many Old Fashioneds are, this is an outstanding drink. The orange peel provides plenty of fruit accent.

2 ounces Old Forester Signature
¼ ounces brown sugar syrup
2 dashes Angostura bitters

Shake all ingredients and pour into a glass filled with ice. Garnish with orange peel.

A COUPLE OF ORIGINAL CREATIONS
FROM CAPTAIN JULIE

Louisvillian Julie Bartlett is a friend of Susan's and a pilot for United Parcel Service. She is also a serious bourbon enthusiast. Julie loves to experiment with cocktails and submitted these simple, and simply delicious, drinks for the book.

JULIE'S NEW MAN(HATTAN), OR MIKE

The Black Label has some caramel and toffee notes, which work well with the maple and black walnut flavors. The Punt e Mes adds a bit of spiciness. This is a great autumn cocktail, since it uses evocative late-season flavors.

1½ ounces Jim Beam Black Label
½ ounce Knob Creek Maple Smoked bourbon or similar product
½ ounce Punt e Mes
A few shakes of black walnut bitters

Shake with ice and pour neat (or add more ice if desired).

JULIE'S ORANGE CREAMSICLE

This drink was inspired by the creamy and citrus finish of Russell's Reserve. The vodka and liqueur are both sweet, so you may want to reduce their amounts if you like your cocktails less sweet. The bitters offset the sweetness nicely. As Julie says, "I'm a heavy-handed bitters girl."

1½ ounces Russell's Reserve
½ ounce whipped cream–flavored vodka
1½ ounces orange-flavored liqueur
A few shakes of orange bitters

Shake with ice and pour neat or over ice.

Maple Bacon Old Fashioned

Beam Me Up, Scotty!

Blackberry Cordial

Kentucky Gimlet

Holiday

Bardstown Cocktail

Kentucky Summer Fruit Punch

Cherry Manhattan

Forester 75

Bourbon Truffle

Pink Berry

Honey Berry

Devil in a Blue Dress

Pineapple Julep

Ginger Snap

Peach Surprise

A COCKTAIL FROM VIRGINIA

Susan's bourbon knowledge is often called upon for tastings across the country. She and Brian Prewitt, the master distiller at A. Smith Bowman Distillery in Fredericksburg, Virginia, have been the bourbon experts for Smithfield, Virginia's annual Bourbon, Bacon & Beach Music Festival, held to raise money for charities in the historic town. Brian shared this recipe for a drink he created for Tales of the Cocktail in New Orleans.

THE REMEDY

1½ ounces of Bowman Brothers Small Batch
½ teaspoon chamomile-infused simple syrup
2 dashes Peychaud's bitters
Ginger ale

Fill the glass halfway with crushed ice. Add the bourbon, syrup, and bitters. Fill to the top with ginger ale and garnish with orange peel.

To make the infused syrup, heat ½ cup sugar and ½ cup water until the sugar dissolves. Add 4 teaspoons dried chamomile and let sit for 5 minutes. Strain, bottle, and refrigerate.

TWO MORE DISTILLERS' COCKTAILS

WILLETT HOLIDAY EGGNOG—THE WILLETT DISTILLERY (BARDSTOWN)

Willett is a small, family-owned distillery located just outside Bardstown. This recipe was provided by one of the owners, Britt Chavanne. You can find more recipes and information about the historic distillery at http://www.kentuckybourbonwhiskey.com.

½ cup Willett Pot Still Reserve
4 cups whole milk
1⅓ cups fine granulated sugar
12 large egg yolks
1 cup chilled heavy whipping cream

In a medium saucepan, whisk milk and sugar over medium heat until sugar is dissolved, 1 to 2 minutes. In a large bowl, whisk egg yolks. Whisking constantly, pour hot mixture into yolks in a slow and steady stream. Return mixture to pan; cook over medium low heat, stirring often, for 20 minutes. Strain into a bowl. Stir in the Willett Pot Still Reserve and cream. Let cool. Cover and refrigerate until chilled. Garnish with a dash of nutmeg, cinnamon, a candy cane (hanging off the rim of the glass), and a cinnamon stick.

MICHTER'S MULE—MICHTER'S DISTILLERY (LOUISVILLE)

2 ounces Michter's US*1 bourbon
¾ ounce sour mix
½ ounce simple syrup
1 ounce ginger beer
Muddled ginger

Muddle fresh ginger and simple syrup. Add ice and the remaining ingredients (except ginger beer). Shake hard and strain into an ice-filled copper mug. Top with ginger beer. Garnish with a lemon wheel and serve with a straw.

BLACK BETTY—MICHTER'S DISTILLERY (LOUISVILLE)

Michter's recently started operating its main distillery in the Shively district of Louisville. The company is also restoring a nineteenth-century building on Whiskey Row on Main Street in Louisville, where it will have a craft distillery and visitors' center. For updates, visit http://www.michters.com.

2 ounces Michter's US*1 bourbon
¾ ounce simple syrup
½ ounce fresh squeezed and strained lemon juice
4 large ripe blackberries

In a cocktail shaker tin, muddle the blackberries to a puree. Add the remaining ingredients, fill with ice, and shake vigorously until well chilled. Strain into a crushed ice–filled Collins or Fancy glass. Garnish with a mint sprig and a large blackberry.

THE WAYSIDER—MICHTER'S DISTILLERY (LOUISVILLE)

1 ounce lime juice

½ ounce simple syrup (2:1 ratio of sugar to water)

2 ounces bourbon (a spicier, high-proof whiskey works best)

1 sprig mint, leaves only

1 ounce ginger beer (we use Fever Tree)

In a tall glass (Collins glass) stir together lime juice, simple syrup, bourbon, and mint leaves. Fill the glass with crushed ice. Top with ginger beer.

CHAPTER THREE

Cocktail Contest Winners

The inspiration for the first Kentucky Bourbon Cocktail Book came from Joy's participation in—and winning of—cocktail contests sponsored by distilleries to showcase their products. Both Joy and Susan have served as judges for numerous cocktail contests, from the Kentucky Bourbon Festival to events held at restaurants and distilleries. In this section we present the winners from three of these contests.

KENTUCKY BOURBON FESTIVAL MIXED-DRINK CHALLENGE

The Kentucky Bourbon Festival takes place in Bardstown in September. The Mixed-Drink Challenge is a cocktail contest that focuses each year on a specific type of bourbon cocktail—for example, Manhattan or julep. The winner is served as the official cocktail of the Kentucky Bourbon Festival the following fall. For more information about the festival, go to http://www.kybourbonfestival.com.

2014 Category—Bourbon Punch

THE RUTLEDGE REBELLION

The cocktail is named for Four Roses master distiller emeritus Jim Rutledge. It was created by Jason Start of Martini Italian Bistro in Louisville, who was representing Four Roses Distillery in the contest.

1½ ounces Four Roses Small Batch

½ ounce ginger liqueur

1 ounce orange juice

1 ounce pomegranate juice

1 ounce apple puree (3 apples, 2 teaspoons salt, 1 cup simple syrup, ½ cup water, and ½ cup lemon juice—blended and strained) *or* 1 ounce apple juice

2 ounces dry champagne

1 syringe Bittermens Tiki bitters

Combine ingredients in a pint glass and stir. Fill with ice, garnish with an orange slice and a mint spring, and serve with a straw.

2012 Category—Old Fashioned

THE OAK FASHIONED

This cocktail is best made in a large batch and aged in a small oak barrel for 3 weeks. That's a little complicated, but the flavor is worth the extra expense and effort. Many large liquor retailers sell oak casks for "home aging."

1½ ounces Kentucky bourbon
½ ounce apple brandy
¼ ounce apple juice
½ ounce dry Curaçao

Combine and shake over ice and strain into a chilled cocktail glass. Garnish with an orange slice and a cherry.

2011 Category—Manhattan

STRAWBERRY FIELDS

2 ounces Kentucky bourbon
1 ounce strawberry syrup
1 ounce Bolin Blanc vermouth
¼ ounce Bonal aperitif

Combine over ice and stir well. Strain into a chilled cocktail glass. Garnish with a strawberry and a mint sprig.

2010 Category—Bourbontini

BLUEGRASS SUNRISE

1¼ ounces Kentucky bourbon
¾ ounce Grand Marnier
4 ounces fresh orange juice
Grenadine

Shake bourbon, Grand Marnier, and orange juice over ice and strain into a chilled cocktail glass. Slowly pour a small amount of grenadine in the center. Garnish with an orange twist and a cherry.

2009 Category—Cobbler

KENTUCKY BOURBON PEACH COBBLER

2 ounces Kentucky bourbon
5 ounces Red Dubonnet
½ fresh peach, chopped
¼ ounce sugar syrup

Combine and shake over ice. Strain into an ice-filled Old Fashioned glass. Garnish with a cinnamon-sprinkled peach slice.

FOUR ROSES' "ROSE JULEP" CONTEST

Each spring Four Roses Distillery sponsors a Rose Julep contest to celebrate the Kentucky Derby, known as the "Run for the Roses" because the winner is draped in a rose blanket. The contest certainly brings out some impressive creativity in Kentucky mixologists.

HONEYSUCKLE ROSE RECIPE

Kyle Tabler, then of Village Anchor, Louisville (he now tends bar at Volare, Louisville), won first place with this recipe in 2012. You will see that you can make this only when honeysuckle is blooming. According to Kyle, "The purpose of the method is that the mint will overwhelm the lavender. Keep them separate until the end and you'll get the essence of both."

2 ounces Four Roses Single Barrel
$\frac{1}{2}$ ounce St. Germain Liqueur
Rosewater
Mint leaves
Crushed ice
$1\frac{1}{2}$ ounces honeysuckle mint syrup
$1\frac{1}{2}$ ounces lavender syrup

Rinse mint julep cup or tall glass with rosewater. Discard rosewater. Add shaved ice. Then top ice with the St. Germain. In a cocktail shaker, add Four Roses Single Barrel and the honeysuckle mint and lavender syrups. Shake and strain into the julep cup. Garnish with mint leaves.

Honeysuckle Mint Syrup (yields 1 quart)
Squeeze 100 honeysuckle blossoms to drip nectar into a pint measuring cup. Add honey to make a pint. Pour into 2-quart saucepan with a pint of water and add 40–50 mint leaves. Bring to a boil. Strain and refrigerate.

Lavender Syrup (yields 1 quart)
Make a simple syrup (1 quart water to 4 cups sugar). Add ½ cup lavender blossoms (available at Whole Foods or other natural foods stores).

BOURBON WOMEN ASSOCIATION—NOT YOUR PINK DRINK CONTEST

Founded in Kentucky in 2011, the Bourbon Women Association now has members in more than thirty states and four countries. Every year it holds an anti-Cosmopolitan contest called "Not Your Pink Drink." The contest is open to both professional and amateur mixologists. The rules stipulate that bourbon must be an ingredient, of course, and there must be at least two other ingredients. (No eggs are allowed.) And the drink must not be pink.

Full disclosure: Susan serves on the board of directors of Bourbon Women and acts as a judge. Joy mixes the drinks for the judging.

Here are some winners from recent years.

2012 *Professional Winner: Rachel Isaacs*

NOT YOUR SUBOURBAN HOUSEWIFE

1 ounce or equal parts of the following:

90-proof bourbon
Butterscotch schnapps
Frangelico hazelnut liquor
Splash Grand Marnier

Shake with ice and strain into a chilled Martini glass rimmed with raw sugar. Garnish with an orange twist and a dried apricot.

2012 Amateur Winner: Karen Rego

HIGH DOLL

1¼ ounces 90-proof bourbon

¾ ounce amaretto

2 ounces chilled lime sparkling water

1 lime wedge

Fill glass with ice. Pour bourbon and amaretto over ice. Add sparkling water. Squeeze juice of lime into glass and add lime wedge. Stir gently. Garnish with an orange slice.

2012 Honorable Mention: Jill Slavinsky

BOURBONISTA APPLE PIE Á LA MODE

2 ounces 80-proof bourbon

¾ ounce apple caramel schnapps

1 ounce sweet cream coffee creamer (or half and half)

Pinch of cinnamon

Place all ingredients in a cocktail shaker filled with ice. Shake well and strain into a chilled Martini glass. Garnish with a cinnamon stick and enjoy.

2013 Professional Winner: Bobby Ridenour,
Rivue Restaurant and Lounge, Louisville

BOURBON SLING

2 ounces Basil Hayden

1 ounce Cointreau

1 whole lemon, freshly squeezed

1 ounce simple syrup

Fill shaker ¾ full of ice. Add all ingredients and shake vigorously 20 times. Strain into a Martini glass. Garnish with a maraschino cherry.

2013 Amateur Winner: Marla Zimmerman, Louisville

PALM BREEZE

1½ ounces Four Roses Single Barrel

2 dashes Peychaud's bitters

1 Splenda packet (¼ teaspoon)

1 slice orange

½ slice grapefruit

1 slice lemon

4 ounces club soda

¾ cup ice

Add the first 3 ingredients to a tall glass and stir until Splenda dissolves. Add the fruit slices—slightly squeeze each to add juice to the mixture. Add club soda, then ice. Use one of the fruit slices on rim of glass as garnish.

2014 Professional Winner: Beth Burrows,
Down One Bourbon Bar, Louisville

DIVA'S ENVY

2 ounces 86.6-proof bourbon
1 ounce Godiva Dark Chocolate Liqueur
½ ounce cinnamon simple syrup
5 drops chocolate bitters

Combine all ingredients except the chocolate bitters; shake with ice. Strain into coupe glass; top with chocolate bitters. Garnish with (egg-free) cookie dough ball around a chocolate straw. Place across glass.

2014 Amateur Winner: Alice Zoeller

KENTUCKY MOON

Grand Marnier
1 ounce 100-proof bourbon (Zoeller notes, "I used Johnny Drum Private Stock")
¼ ounce Frangelico

Coat the inside of a chilled rocks glass with Grand Marnier, discarding the excess. Add the bourbon and Frangelico. Garnish with an orange zest twist.

2015 Professional Winner: Bob Knott, Old Seelbach Bar, Louisville

MINTED GOLD

1½ ounces 80-proof bourbon
1 ounce honey syrup
2 ounces fresh orange juice
2 ounces fresh lemon juice
Ginger beer

Shake all ingredients (except ginger beer) with ice and strain into an Old Fashioned glass. Top with ginger beer and garnish with a mint sprig.

2015 Amateur Winner: Heather Wibbels

THE FRENCH QUARTER MANHATTAN

Heather says, "This cocktail was one of my successes in getting my not-so-bourbon-centric husband to enjoy a bourbon cocktail."

2 ounces 90-proof small-batch bourbon

1 ounce praline liquor

4–5 dashes chocolate bitters

Add all ingredients over ice in a cocktail shaker. Shake vigorously and strain into a chilled cocktail glass. Garnish with a praline or candied pecan.

CHAPTER FOUR

A Bourbon-Inspired Kentucky Buffet

Our friend Albert Schmid has worked as an executive chef and is currently a professor at Sullivan University and the director of the hotel-restaurant management and hospitality management departments at the university's National Center for Hospitality Management. He graciously agreed to let us use some recipes from his award-winning *The Kentucky Bourbon Cookbook* (2010). The descriptive notes at the start of each recipe are Albert's own. He has also written definitive books about the histories of the Old Fashioned and Manhattan cocktails. (See our "Suggested Further Reading" list for details.)

If you are planning a brunch, lunch, or dinner buffet for a crowd, these dishes will fit the occasion. Add a platter of Kentucky-made cheeses, crackers, and some fruit and you are all set.

Accent your meal with bourbon-based drinks made by the pitcher: Bardstown Cocktail (p. 2), Pineapple Punch (pp. 2–3), Ginger Snap (pp. 4–5), and Summer Manhattan (p. 17). All will pair beautifully with the buffet. Pour each into ice-filled glasses so you do not water down the cocktails in the pitchers and ruin your drink.

PORK TENDERLOIN IN SPICED APPLE KENTUCKY BOURBON SAUCE

Pork and apple are a classic combination that every chef learns early in his or her career. Here the apple is in the form of juice, flavored and thickened to form a sauce for the pork. This recipe, which comes from A Love Affair with Southern Cooking, *by Jean Anderson (New York: HarperCollins, 2007), could easily be served with sweet potatoes (also traditionally combined with pork and bourbon) or with a rice pilaf.*

6 servings

3 pounds boned rolled pork loin
1/2 teaspoon freshly ground pepper
2 tablespoons spicy brown mustard
1 cup apple juice
1/4 cup Kentucky bourbon
1 1/4 cups plus 1/2 cup chicken broth
1/2 cup half and half
5 tablespoons all-purpose flour
1/2 teaspoon salt

1. Rub the pork with the pepper and place in a medium roasting pan. Mix the mustard, apple juice, and bourbon until smooth. Brush the pork with the mixture and let stand for 30 minutes at room temperature. While it rests, preheat the oven to 425 degrees. Baste the pork with the bourbon mixture again, and place the pork in the preheated oven for 45 minutes or until the pork reaches an internal temperature of 150 degrees.

2. To make the sauce: Deglaze the roasting pan with the remaining bourbon mixture; then pour the deglazing mixture into a saucepan and boil for 2 minutes. Stir in the 1¼ cups chicken broth and the half and half. Mix the ½ cup broth with the flour and salt, add the flour mixture to the saucepan, and mix. Cook over medium heat until the mixture thickens.

3. Slice the pork and serve with mashed potatoes and the apple-bourbon sauce.

KENTUCKY BOURBON BEEF TENDERLOIN

Beef tenderloin is very lean and very tender. This recipe combines ingredients to form a sweet and sour sauce for the meat. The addition of a baked sweet potato complements the sweet flavors of the sauce, while a baked white potato helps foil the sweet and sour flavors.

6 servings

1 cup Kentucky bourbon
1¼ cup brown sugar
²/₃ cup soy sauce
1 cup finely chopped cilantro
½ cup lemon juice
2 tablespoons Worcestershire sauce
2 cups water
1 teaspoon dried thyme
4 pounds beef tenderloin

Combine the bourbon, brown sugar, soy sauce, cilantro, lemon juice, Worcestershire sauce, water, and thyme to make a marinade. Cut the beef tenderloin into 2-inch slices and pour the marinade over them. Allow the beef to marinate, refrigerated, for at least 2 hours (for best results, marinate for up to 6 hours). Turn it at least every hour to allow equal marinating for each piece. Preheat the oven to 350 degrees and cook the tenderloin in the oven until done (the meat should be pink inside), about 20 minutes. Cut into serving-size pieces.

KENTUCKY COLONEL BOURBON BALLS

Bourbon balls are a classic winter confection. In The Art of Southern Cooking *(New York: Gramercy Books, 2003), Mildred Evans Warren creates a bourbon ball that does not utilize old cake as some recipes do. Instead she combines pecans, butter, and confectioners' sugar with bourbon and covers the sweet treat with chocolate. She names it after the Kentucky Colonels.*

8 servings

1 cup pecan halves plus additional for garnish
¼ cup Kentucky bourbon
1 pound confectioners' sugar
½ cup butter
1 teaspoon vanilla extract
4 ounces (4 squares) bittersweet chocolate
1 tablespoon melted paraffin

1. Soak the 1 cup of pecans in bourbon for several hours. Mix the sugar, butter, and vanilla until creamy. Drain the pecans, reserving the bourbon liquid that remains; mix the liquid into the sugar mixture.
2. Roll the sugar mixture into marble-size balls around the pecan halves. Chill the balls in the refrigerator for 1 hour.
3. Melt the chocolate and add the paraffin. Dip the cooled balls into the melted chocolate; use a fork to retrieve the balls from the melted chocolate mixture. Top each ball with a pecan half and allow to dry.

KENTUCKY BOURBON CHICKEN WINGS

Another appetizer that's great for Derby is chicken wings—but then they are the perfect appetizer all year long. This is a simple dish, as easy to prepare as it is to eat.

6 servings

24 chicken wings with skin
¼ cup Kentucky bourbon
2 tablespoons olive oil
1 tablespoon finely chopped lemon zest
3 tablespoons lemon juice (the juice of 1 lemon)
1 cup fine, dry bread crumbs, unseasoned
1 tablespoon sweet Hungarian paprika
Salt and pepper

1. Cut each wing into three pieces. Discard the wing tips or save them for chicken stock. Combine the wing pieces, bourbon, olive oil, lemon zest, and lemon juice in a bowl. Toss to coat the wings, and marinate them for at least 2 hours in the refrigerator.

CANDIED KENTUCKY BOURBON-BACON BITES

This simple recipe is adapted from Paula Deen's The Deen Family Cookbook *(New York: Simon & Schuster, 2009), by the "Dean of Southern Cuisine." Deen is a native of Georgia but has a connection to Kentucky through her appearance as Aunt Dora in the Cameron Crowe movie* Elizabethtown.

20 servings

¾ pound bacon
2 tablespoons Kentucky bourbon
½ cup packed light brown sugar

1. Preheat the oven to 350 degrees. Select a baking sheet that has a lip, and line it with foil; place a wire rack on the foil. Arrange the bacon strips close together in a single layer on the rack, brush them with the bourbon, and sprinkle the brown sugar over them.
2. Bake the bacon until crisp and dark golden brown, 20 to 25 minutes. Transfer the bacon strips to a wire rack set over another baking sheet with a lip or lay them on a paper towel-lined plate, to cool slightly. Break each strip in half and serve warm or at room temperature.

ANGELS' SHARE BISCUITS

When bourbon (or any other distilled spirit) comes off the still, it is as clear as water. The color and flavor of bourbon develop as it ages in a burned or toasted oak barrel. During the aging process, some of the bourbon is lost to evaporation, and this evaporated alcohol is called the "Angels' share" by the distilling and wine-making industry. As the biscuit bakes, the alcohol evaporates to the angels, but the bourbon flavor stays behind in the biscuit. In the United States a biscuit is a roll made with chemical leavening such as baking soda or baking powder. An Angel biscuit, made with yeast and/or the chemical leavening, is half biscuit, half roll. These Angel biscuits made with bourbon can be served with most meals.

Yield: 2 dozen biscuits

½ cup warm water
3 tablespoons honey
1 tablespoon yeast
5 cups flour
1 teaspoon baking soda
1 teaspoon baking powder
1 teaspoon salt
½ cup butter
½ cup shortening
1½ cup buttermilk
¼ cup Kentucky bourbon

1. Preheat the oven to 400 degrees. Mix the warm water and honey together and dissolve the yeast in the water-honey mixture.
2. In a separate bowl, mix the flour, baking soda, baking powder, and salt. Add the butter and shortening and mix with a pastry blender until the mixture resembles fine cornmeal.
3. Mix the buttermilk and bourbon with the yeast mixture; add these ingredients to the flour mixture. Combine lightly until the ingredients are just mixed together.
4. Grease a baking pan and drop mounds of dough onto it. Bake for 10 minutes or until golden brown.

KENTUCKY BOURBON BROWNIES

Brownies are one of Americans' favorite confections. If you especially like the edges of brownies, you might want to buy an Edge Brownie Pan, which allows each slice of the brownies to develop a slightly crusty edge. The pan, invented by 2002 Sullivan University graduate Emily Griffin, has been featured in many magazines, including Fine Cooking *and* Good Housekeeping. *These brownies are made with bourbon-flavored pecans.*

9 servings

½ cup chopped pecans
¾ cup Kentucky bourbon
½ cup butter
½ cup margarine
10 ounces (10 squares) semisweet chocolate

1 cup granulated sugar

½ cup brown sugar, firmly packed

½ teaspoon salt

5 eggs

¼ cup unsweetened cocoa

1½ cups flour

1. Preheat the oven to 350 degrees. Place the pecans and bourbon in a small bowl, so that the pecans will absorb the bourbon. After about 30 minutes, or when the bourbon is reduced by about half, remove the pecans to a small baking sheet and reserve the remaining bourbon. Toast the pecans in the oven for about 5 minutes.

2. Heat the butter, margarine, and chocolate in a double boiler until melted together. Remove the pan containing the butter-chocolate mixture from the hot water and allow the mixture to cool to room temperature. Add the sugar, brown sugar, salt, eggs, and reserved bourbon. Whisk until the ingredients are well mixed. Add the cocoa and mix until it is totally incorporated. Stir in the flour and the pecans.

3. Apply nonstick spray to an 8 × 8–inch pan and pour in the batter. Bake for about 25 minutes or until a toothpick comes out clean. Cut the brownies when they are cool.

KENTUCKY BIBB SALAD WITH A SWEET KENTUCKY BOURBON VINAIGRETTE, CRUMBLED GOAT CHEESE, AND TOASTED PECANS

This salad is a great summer dish because of the cool, seasonal ingredients. The recipe calls for Bibb lettuce, also known as limestone lettuce, which was first cultivated in Kentucky by Jack Bibb in the late 1800s. Bibb lettuce is highly prized by chefs and gourmands. I based this recipe on one I found in the 2003 edition of Nancy Miller's Secrets of Louisville Chefs *(Louisville: Tobe).*

4 servings

Kentucky Bibb Salad
1 cup pecan halves
3 heads Bibb lettuce, washed and patted dry
12 heirloom tomatoes or two large tomatoes
12 red grape tomatoes
½ pound goat cheese
1 red onion, diced

Sweet Kentucky Bourbon Vinaigrette
¼ cup cider vinegar
2½ tablespoons Kentucky bourbon
¼ cup brown mustard
2 tablespoons honey
2 tablespoons barbecue sauce
1½ teaspoons freshly ground pepper
1½ teaspoons garlic chili sauce

A Bourbon-Inspired Kentucky Buffet

1. Toast the pecans. Preheat the oven to 350 degrees, spread the pecans on a baking sheet, and toast them for about 5 minutes.
2. *To make the salad:* Break the lettuce apart, cut all the tomatoes in half or in slices, and break or slice the goat cheese.
3. *To make the vinaigrette:* Mix the vinegar, bourbon, mustard, honey, barbecue sauce, pepper, and chili sauce together.
4. Arrange lettuce, tomatoes, onions, pecans, and cheese on four plates, and pour the vinaigrette over the salad.

DRUNKEN VIDALIAS

Vidalia onions, when available in the spring and summer, are easy to add to the grill to make a hearty, tasty side dish to accompany anything from fish to chicken to beef. Here, the famous southern sweetie gets a little tipsy on the grill with a hearty dose of bourbon.

4 servings

4 large Vidalia onions
Garlic salt
Pepper
1 cup butter, melted
¼ cup Kentucky bourbon
¼ cup brown sugar
1 tablespoon balsamic vinegar

Note: *If you are using coals, be sure to start the grill at least 1 hour before you want to grill the onions.*

1. Cut a thin slice off the bottom, or root end, of each Vidalia onion, so that the onions can stand upright. Remove the outer skins and core the onions almost to the base, creating cavities about 2 inches wide. Spray the outside surfaces of the onions with nonstick spray, then (using the garlic salt) salt and pepper the sprayed surfaces. Place each onion on a large piece of aluminum foil, and salt and pepper the cavities as well.

2. Mix the melted butter, bourbon, brown sugar, and balsamic vinegar in a bowl and fill the cavities with the butter mixture. Reserve the remaining butter mixture. Gather the foil around each onion at the top and twist to seal the onion. Cook the wrapped onions over indirect heat on the grill for 1 hour and 30 minutes. To achieve indirect heat, allow the coals to stop burning and just glow. Also, place the onions off to one side of the grill. Remove the onions from the foil, warm up the reserved butter mix, and drizzle it over the Vidalias just before serving.

KENTUCKY TOMATO BOURBON SOUP

This recipe is a summer offering shared by chef David Dodd, who from 1968 to 1975 served as the special commitment chef in the kitchens of the British royal family.

4 servings

4 tablespoons butter
2 onions, chopped
4 pounds Roma tomatoes, peeled, seeded, and chopped
4 carrots, chopped
1 quart chicken stock
4 tablespoons chopped parsley
1 tablespoon chopped thyme
Salt and pepper
½ cup Kentucky bourbon
½ cup heavy cream
4 sprigs thyme for garnish

Melt the butter in a large saucepan. Add the onions and cook for 5 minutes until soft. Stir in the tomatoes, carrots, chicken stock, parsley, and thyme. Bring to a simmer, cover the pan, and cook for 20 minutes. Puree the soup in a blender until smooth. Return the pureed soup to the pan, season it with salt and pepper, and add the bourbon. Stir in the cream and reheat slowly (do not boil), and garnish with thyme.

KENTUCKY BOURBON BAKED BEANS

What is a good barbecue without baked beans?

4 servings

6 strips bacon
1 (28-ounce) can pork and beans
1/3 cup Kentucky bourbon
1 large onion, chopped
1/4 cup brown sugar
1 tablespoon ketchup
1 teaspoon brown mustard
1 tablespoon lemon juice

Preheat the oven to 350 degrees. Fry the bacon until cooked but not crisp and set it aside. Combine the beans, bourbon, onion, brown sugar, ketchup, mustard, and lemon juice in a large ovenproof pot. Bake for 45 minutes or until warmed through. Top the beans with the bacon.

KENTUCKY BOURBON APPLE PIE

This recipe combines America's native spirit with the all-American dessert.

6 servings

¹/₂ cup Kentucky bourbon

¹/₂ cup raisins

10 Granny Smith apples

³/₄ cup sugar

2 tablespoons flour

1 teaspoon cinnamon

¹/₄ teaspoon salt

¹/₈ teaspoon nutmeg

¹/₂ cup pecan halves, toasted

1 double piecrust

1 tablespoon superfine sugar

1. Combine the bourbon and raisins; let soak for at least 1 hour.
2. Preheat the oven to 350 degrees.
3. Peel the apples and slice them thinly. Sauté the apple slices in a pan with a little butter until tender. Meanwhile, toast the pecans in the oven for about 5 minutes.
4. Combine the sugar, flour, cinnamon, salt, and nutmeg in a large bowl and mix. Add the apples, raisin mixture, and pecans. Spoon the pie filling into the bottom of a 10-inch piecrust.

5. Cut the top piecrust into strips and arrange the strips over the pie filling in a lattice formation. Sprinkle the pie with the superfine sugar and bake it at 350 degrees until the filling in the center of the pie bubbles, about 1 hour and 15 minutes. Allow the pie to cool for at least 15 minutes before serving.

SWEET POTATOES WITH KENTUCKY BOURBON

This is a great side dish to serve at the Thanksgiving table with the traditional turkey. I found the recipe in Splendor in the Bluegrass *(2000), a book compiled by the Junior League of Louisville. Kentucky bourbon adds a new dimension to the sweet potatoes and results in a classic pairing.*

6 servings

5 pounds sweet potatoes, unpeeled
¼ cup heavy cream
1 tablespoon fresh lemon juice
½ teaspoon freshly grated lemon zest
Salt and pepper
⅓ cup Kentucky bourbon
¼ cup dark brown sugar

1. Preheat the oven to 450 degrees. Pierce the sweet potatoes with a fork and place them in a large roasting pan. Roast them for 1 hour or until tender. Remove them from the oven and allow them to stand for at least 15 to 30 minutes before proceeding.

2. Peel the sweet potatoes and cut them into large chunks. Combine the sweet potatoes with the cream, lemon juice, and lemon zest in a mixing bowl. Add the salt and pepper to taste. Using an electric mixer, mash the sweet potato mixture.

3. Combine the bourbon and brown sugar in a large saucepan and heat to a boil. Stir the sweet potato mixture into the bourbon mixture and cook, stirring occasionally, over low heat until heated through.

ACKNOWLEDGMENTS

From Joy:

Thanks to all the Kentucky bourbon distilleries, large and small, for producing this great spirit we call bourbon. Thanks to chef Dean Corbett, with whom I've worked for thirty years at Equus and Jack's Lounge, for giving me the opportunity to make and serve my bourbon cocktails. Thanks to my daughter, Melissa, my other pair of hands, who gets me where I need to be and helps me to do what I do.

Thanks to the Kentucky Bourbon Festival in Bardstown for inviting me to be a judge in the Mixed-Drink Challenge and giving me my own event—Kentucky Bourbon Mixology—year after year. I love you! Thanks to Susan Reigler for asking me if I would like to write a bourbon cocktail book. And thanks to the thousands of people from all over America and the world who love Kentucky bourbon as much as I do.

I hope everyone enjoys reading this book and making the cocktails. And please drink responsibly!

From Susan:

Many thanks to all the bartenders, restaurant managers, and others who provided recipes for the cocktails in chapters 2 and 3. Also many thanks to Albert Schmid for allowing us to use recipes from *The Kentucky Bourbon Cookbook*. (There are so many more: if you enjoyed this sampling, do get a copy of his cookbook.)

In the interval between the publication of the first *Kentucky Bourbon Cocktail Book* and this volume, there has been an explosion of activity by bartenders all over America, not just in Kentucky, creating wonderful bourbon cocktails. I credit Joy Perrine with leading the trend. She has been an inspiration to a new generation of bourbon mixologists. Thank you, Joy, for allowing me to help bring your creations to print.

Cheers!

APPENDIX

Adapted from *The Kentucky Bourbon Cocktail Book*, "Getting Started"

EQUIPMENT NEEDED

Shakers

Standard shaker made of stainless steel or chrome, *or*

Boston shaker, which has a stainless steel top half that fits over a glass bottom half or a drink glass. (Most home bartenders find the standard shaker easier to use.)

It is very important to have a large shaker with room for lots of ice; at least four or five large cubes should take up only about half of your shaker's volume. In the recipes that call for shaking, don't be afraid to be enthusiastic. If your shaker frosts up, you are doing it right. Of course, you'll be more comfortable holding the shaker with a towel during this process.

Measurers

4-ounce measured shot glass

Glass measuring cup

Strainer

Hawthorn bar strainer, flat, with a steel coil

You can find these in any kitchenware shop that carries bar supplies. The strainer fits over the rim of the glass. Pour the chilled contents of the shaker into the glass.

Muddler

A small wooden pestle used for crushing fruit and "muddling" it, as the name suggests, with water and/or sugar

Long-handled Spoon

Great for stirring pitchers of drinks. Have both metal and wooden spoons on hand.

Zester/Channel Knife

This is the gizmo you use to get twists of fruit peel, such as lemon or orange.

Glasses

Most of the recipes in this book call for either an Old Fashioned (also called rocks) glass or a cocktail (also called Martini) glass. A few need other types. The following icons indicate the glass required for each recipe:

⊔	Old Fashioned	Y	Cordial
Y	Cocktail	⊔	Julep
⊔	Tall	◡	Punch
⍩	Champagne flute	◯	Snifter
⍙	Wineglass	⊤	Coupe
⊔	Pint	⊔	Mason jar
⊔	Half pint	⊔	Copper mug

BOURBON TERMINOLOGY

You'll be able to "speak bourbon" like an expert when you know the language. These are the terms you will encounter on bourbon labels.

Aging: Bourbon must be aged in charred, never-before-used barrels made of white oak (*Quercus alba*) for at least two years to be called straight bourbon. If the bourbon is aged fewer than four years, the label must state the age, for example, "thirty-six months."

Bourbon: Whiskey distilled from fermented grain. By law, at least 51 percent of the mash bill (grains used) must be corn. Other grains used are typically barley and rye, in varying proportions. Wheat is sometimes used in place of rye; such whiskeys are called "wheated" bourbons.

The name *bourbon* is said by some to come from Bourbon County, Kentucky, named to honor the French royal family that aided the American colonists during the War for Independence. The true origin remains a mystery.

Proof: Equal to twice the alcohol content by volume. Hence, an 86-proof bourbon is 43 percent alcohol. Proofs are adjusted by the addition of water after aging. A **barrel proof** or **cask strength bourbon** has not been so adjusted. These are typically 110 proof and higher.

Single barrel: The bottling is all from one selected barrel. Yield: 65–120 bottles, depending on evaporation during aging.

Small batch: A limited production of bourbon using select mixed barrels. This might be two barrels or as many as several dozen. There is no rule about this.

Sour mash: The soupy alcoholic liquid strained from the first distillation and added to the next batch of grain for distillation (rather like a sourdough starter). Also called **backset.** Dr. James Crow, a Scot who came to Kentucky in 1826, used the technique to help keep bourbon consistent from one distillation to the next. The first written description of the process was made in 1818 by Kentucky farmer Catherine Spears Frye Carpenter.

Straight bourbon whiskey: The legal definition of American bourbon says that "straight bourbon" is made up of at least 51 percent corn; is distilled at no more than 80 percent alcohol; is matured at no higher than 62.5 percent alcohol; and is matured in new charred oak barrels for at least two years. It is bottled at a minimum of 40 percent alcohol by volume.

Whiskey (spelled "whisky" in Europe): An alcoholic beverage made from distilled grain. Bourbon is one of many whiskeys, including Scotch, Canadian, Irish, rye, Tennessee, and Kentucky whiskey. The last differs from bourbon in being aged in *used* charred oak barrels.

SUGGESTED FURTHER READING

These books will give you more information on cocktail mixing in general and bourbon and its history in particular. It is by no means an exhaustive list, but these are books we particularly like.

Broom, Dave. *New American Bartender's Handbook.* San Diego: Thunder Bay, 2003.

DeGroff, Dale. *The Craft of the Cocktail.* New York: Clarkson Potter, 2002.

Herbst, Sharon Tyler, and Ron Herbst. *The Ultimate A-to-Z Bar Guide.* New York: Broadway Books, 1998.

Minnick, Fred. *Whiskey Women: The Untold Story of How Women Saved Bourbon, Scotch, and Irish Whiskey.* Lincoln, NE: Potomac Books, 2013.

Nickell, Col. Joe. *The Kentucky Mint Julep.* Lexington: University Press of Kentucky, 2003.

Perrine, Joy, and Susan Reigler. *The Kentucky Bourbon Cocktail Book.* Lexington: University Press of Kentucky, 2009.

Poister, John J. *The New American Bartender's Guide.* New York: New American Library, 1999.

Regan, Gary. *The Joy of Mixology: The Consummate Guide to the Bartender's Craft.* New York: Clarkson Potter, 2003.

Reigler, Susan, and Michael Veach. *The Bourbon Tasting Notebook.* Morley, MO: Acclaim, 2015.

Schmid, Albert W. A. *The Kentucky Bourbon Cookbook.* Lexington: University Press of Kentucky, 2010.

——. *The Manhattan Cocktail: A Modern Guide to the Whiskey Classic.* Lexington: University Press of Kentucky, 2015.

——. *The Old Fashioned: An Essential Guide to the Original Whiskey Cocktail.* Lexington: University Press of Kentucky, 2013.

Thomas, Jerry. *The Bar-tender's Guide: How to Mix Drinks.* 1887. Reprint, Seattle: CreateSpace, 2008.

Veach, Michael R. *Kentucky Bourbon Whiskey: An American Heritage.* Lexington: University Press of Kentucky, 2013.

Wellmann, Molly. *Handcrafted Cocktails: The Mixologist's Guide to Classic Drinks for Morning, Noon & Night.* Cincinnati: Betterway Home, 2013.

Williams, H. I. *3 Bottle Bar.* New York: M. S. Mill, 1946.

INDEX

bitters *(cont.)*

    chocolate, in French Quarter Manhattan, 56

    cranberry, in Holiday Cocktail, 7

    grapefruit, in Grapefruit Old Fashioned, 6

    lemon, in Honey of a Manhattan, 24

    lemon, in New Fashioned #2, 14

    Old Fashioned, in Bulleit-Vardier, 34

    plum, in Pineapple Plum Old Fashioned, 13

    rhubarb, in Strawberry Rhubarb Old Fashioned, 12

    Tiki, in The Rutledge Rebellion, 46

    See also Angostura bitters; orange bitters;
        Peychaud's bitters; Woodford Reserve Spiced
        Cherry Bitters

blackberries

    Black Betty, 43–44

    Charr'd Blackberry Manhattan, 29

Blackberry Cordial, 4

blackberry-infused bourbon, in Blackberry
   Cordial, 4

Blackberry Manhattan, Charr'd, 29

blackberry syrup

    Blackberry Cordial, 4

    Honey Berry, 6

Black Betty, 43–44

Black Cherry Bounce, 22

Blanford, Evan, 38

blood orange soda, in Heller in Pink Tights, 32

blueberries

    Blueberry Orange Old Fashioned, 13

    Kentucky Summer Fruit Punch, 18

blueberry juice

    Blueberry Twist, 21–22

    Devil in a Blue Dress, 5

Blueberry Orange Old Fashioned, 13

blueberry syrup, in Blueberry Orange Old
   Fashioned, 13

Blueberry Twist, 21–22

Bluegrass Sunrise, 48

Bonal aperitif, in Strawberry Fields, 47

bourbon, 1

    See also specific brands

Bourbon, Bacon & Beach Music Festival
   (Smithfield, Virginia), 41

Bourbon Balls, Kentucky Colonel, 61

Bourbon Barrel Foods (Louisville, Kentucky),
   vii–viii, 7

bourbon-based product recipes, 21–25

Bourbon Cocktail Mixology program, 2, 4

Bourbonista Apple Pie á la Mode, 52

Bourbons Bistro (Louisville, Kentucky), 28

Bourbon Sling, 53

Bourbon Truffle, 25

Bourbon Women Association, 51–56

Bowman Brothers Small Batch, in The Remedy, 41

Brown-Forman Distillery (Louisville, Kentucky),
   2–3, 26, 34

Brownies, Kentucky Bourbon, 65–66

Brown Sugar Old Fashioned, 39

brown sugar syrup

    Black Cherry Bounce, 22

ABOUT THE AUTHORS

Joy Perrine is a native of New Jersey, but that hasn't stopped her from developing an abiding love of Kentucky bourbon. She has been named "Best Bartender in Louisville" by *Louisville Magazine* and has won numerous awards for her cocktails. Articles about her and her drinks recipes have appeared in the *Louisville Courier-Journal*, *Southern Living*, and at www.southernfoodways.com. She is the bar manager emerita at Equus and Jack's Lounge in Louisville.

Susan Reigler is an award-winning former restaurant critic and drinks writer for the *Louisville Courier-Journal*. Her articles about bourbon have been published in *Malt Advocate* and *Wine Enthusiast* as well as in several books about traveling in Kentucky. She is the author of *Kentucky Bourbon Country: The Essential Travel Guide* and coauthor, with Michael Veach, of *The Bourbon Tasting Notebook*. She lives in Louisville and has served on the board of directors, including as president, of the Bourbon Women Association.